Expectations Ruin Relationships

By Mark Foster

All Scripture quotations are taken from the King James Bible

Dedication:

I want to dedicate this book to my loving wife, who has often had to hear these principles as I worked them out in my head. She is more than I could have ever expected!

Table of Contents

Preface

The Idea for this book came out of my experience as a pastor, husband, father, and friend. In reality, the title came to me one day while trying to deal with a very difficult situation with a member of my church. I had not lived up to their expectations, and they were considering leaving our church. While seeking counsel from an advisor, I made the statement which led to a sermon, which led to a series, which led to this book. I said, "Do you know what the problem is? The problem is their expectations. Their expectations are ruining this relationship."

That is how the idea was born. From that time to this a few years have gone by. Whenever I would mention this principle, or have the occasion to speak on this subject in my own church, or at another church I would receive a terrific amount of feedback: all positive. The principles set forth in the next few pages are not difficult to understand. Applying them, however, will be one of the greatest challenges of your life. Trust me, I have had to try and apply them to my own life. I am still trying! + HE WROTE THE BOOK?

I can say with certainty that when applied, the principles of this book have made better every relationship I have. They have helped me as a Pastor to salvage marriages and relationships. They just work! My prayer and desire is that you would find the strength to apply what you are about to read to your own life. That is reward enough for any author.

Let me give you one final word of explanation. This book is not dealing with professional relationships, such as boss/employee. Of course an employer has a right to expect certain things from their employees. The relationships mentioned in this book are personal relationships. Understanding that may help you to better grasp the concepts I will present.

Introduction

Have you ever had a ruined relationship? Are you in the middle of a difficult relationship right now, wondering if there is any hope? There is hope! You can build lasting, happy relationships. The problem standing between you and this goal is in most cases one word: EXPECTATIONS. Not what you expected? As you read this book I want you to know that if you apply the truth found in its pages to your relationship you will see a drastic change for the good. I promise this based on my own relationship experiences and the testimony of those who have applied this principle to their relationships. This book will not fix the other person. At the risk of having you put the book down now I must tell you that the other person is not the problem. The problem is your expectations, and as you will come to understand, <u>expectations ruin relationships</u>.

Chapter One – Conditioned to Expect

- "Be careful the environment you choose for it will shape you; be careful the friends you choose for you will become like them."-
-W. Clement Stone

Conditioned by Society

We've all seen her, the sweet little angel at the grocery store. You may have seen her on the cereal aisle, or perhaps at the checkout counter. She is such a darling little girl! With a sweet face and big beautiful eyes she turns to her mother.

"I want this." She says sweetly, or not.

You know what happens next. If the mother says yes then there is no problem. However, if that mother dares to say no, it's all over. All of a sudden, that sweet little girl, who a moment ago was happy, is transformed into a demonic little beast kicking and screaming and making her mother wonder why she ever had children! Sound like anyone you know?

You may wonder how this can happen. One moment the girl was happy and the next she was not so happy. What changed? I will tell you. Her expectations were not met. She expected her Mother to give her what she wanted. Her mother did not live up to those expectations, and so the relationship is in trouble. Sadly many children never grow out of this attitude of expectation.

We live in a society that has conditioned us to place expectations upon those with whom we are in a relationship. How has it done this? Take a look at the television, music, and other media we are consuming from a very young age. It is almost entirely designed to condition us to expect. We are told what to expect from our future mate, from our parents, from society, from sex- and the list goes on. When we find that "perfect" mate, and then they do not live up to our expectations, we trash the relationship rather than the expectations. When we graduate from high school and the world does not bow before us, we grow bitter and demand a handout. We claim this is our right, because society has let us down! Why do we think society has let us down? We have been conditioned to do so!

[handwritten margin note: THIS IS WHAT U WANT ME TO BE.]

At the time of this writing, the term you may hear most often from politicians is the word *entitlement*. This is just another word for expectations. People have been conditioned to expect certain things from the Government, and when those expectations are not met, there is trouble. Someone expects the Government to pay for healthcare, or groceries, or college, or whatever. Why? They have been conditioned to do so!

As a Pastor I see this attitude all the time. Sometimes it seems that the problems I face in counseling are directly related to unmet expectations. Where did these expectations come from? In almost all cases, they came from the society in which that particular person was raised. Wives whose fathers were always home at 6:15 for dinner expect their husbands to do the same. In most cases, it never enters their minds

[handwritten note at bottom: U EXPECTED UR DAD TO ABUSE YOU SO WHEN I DIDN'T YOU STILL WERE EXPECTING IT. NEVER CAME.]

that it could be any other way. They have been conditioned to expect it, and therefore it must be so. Husbands whose mothers got up each morning to fix them a hot breakfast may be upset with a wife who places a box of cereal in front of them after they are married. He was expecting her to behave like he was accustomed to the woman of the house behaving. *WRONG!*

We often do not mind someone exceeding our expectations, but we are not likely to compliment them for doing so. However, when someone does not live up to the expectations we have been conditioned to have, we make a scene, much like that little girl in the grocery store aisle. You may think I am kidding, but I have had people sit on my couch during a counseling session upset over just such trivial things as these. To them they weren't trivial. To them they were unmet expectations. They felt robbed, cheated, and let down. The relationship is on the rocks, and all because of expectations.

Conditioned by Our Sin Nature

You and I may not like to admit it, but we were born with a sin nature. This sin nature begins very early in our lives to tell us that others exist to serve us. Whatever we want, others should provide. Why? We are selfish. Selfishness is a sin. We were born with this sin nature that tips the scales in the direction of selfishness and expectations. We are looking out for good old number one!

As I counsel with people I find that even those with new life in Christ still struggle with expectations.

Is it any wonder that so many marriages end in divorce? Is it any wonder that so many church members get angry and leave their church? We go into these, and other relationships with an old nature that tells us to expect to be served. When our expectations are not met, we assume wrongdoing on the part of others, and the relationship is ruined!

The Bible says in **Philippians 2:3 Let nothing be done through strife or vainglory; but in lowliness of mind let each esteem other better than themselves.** Now I don't know about you dear friend, but I do not naturally esteem others ahead of myself. On the contrary, I naturally assume that my needs and desires come first. Why? I have been conditioned to do so!

Ephesians 5:29 For no man ever yet hated his own flesh; but nourisheth and cherisheth it...

Did you notice how it is natural that we cherish ourselves? Our selfish nature is going to make sure we get what we need. If this attitude is not overcome, it will ruin every relationship we begin. No relationship can last and be healthy without someone willing to serve the other first. That is unnatural! WHEN I STOPPED, U LEFT.

Every relationship I have is an opportunity to serve others. Why does it then seem that so many people are upset that others are not living up to their expectations? Have you ever stopped to think about how much you expect from your spouse? How about your church family or your Pastor? Take a moment right now, and realize how selfish we are prone to be.

The last time you had an argument with your

spouse, is it at least possible that the argument had to do with someone not living up to expectations? Are you getting the picture? We are conditioned by society and our sin nature to be *expect-ers*. We are good at it. Expecting feels so natural. It feels so right! There is only one problem. Expectations ruin relationships!

+ MAKE SURE THEY STAY THAT WAY.

At the end of this chapter you will have some questions to answer before going on to the next chapter. If you will do so honestly, you will be better prepared to move on and accept what you will read in later chapters. You will need to be honest with yourself. You will need to ask God to show you the truth about your relationships. Really, it is not that difficult. It is, however, humbling.

Choose Your Environment Carefully

The Bible is careful to warn us about the environment we choose. Read these verses carefully:

Proverbs 13:20 ¶ He that walketh with wise men shall be wise: but a companion of fools shall be destroyed.

Proverbs 22:24 ¶ Make no friendship with an angry man; and with a furious man thou shalt not go:

1Corinthians 15:33 Be not deceived: evil communications corrupt good manners.

Have you ever wondered what makes one person hold to certain political and social views? When you listen to the political discourse you will walk away with the impression that both sides believe they are right. Why does one person believe in individual responsibility and limited government and another believe that it is the government's job to take care of every need of the individual? These beliefs are a product of the environment in which a person grew up. Our experiences and environment shape our expectations.

A woman who is the victim of an abusive husband may develop the belief and expectation that all men are monsters. These expectations will ruin any good relationship she could have with another man. I am not blaming her, just stating the danger. The same is true of children in the foster care system. Some find good homes and have a good experience, while others are passed from home to home and develop the expectation of rejection. Soon they are unable to bond with their newest foster parents because they expect them to be just like the last ones. These expectations ruin relationships.

I realize that in the last two illustrations, the people involved may have had no choice in their environment; I used them to prove the point that environments affect expectations. We ought to be very careful when choosing the environment we place ourselves in to the extent that it is our choice. Carefully consider your choice of a mate, a church, a neighborhood, etc. We are products of the environments in which we exist.

Personal Application:

Read the following questions carefully. Take

time to think about them before giving your answers. After completing the answers, take some time to read and meditate on the passage of Scripture found below. Ask God to show you where you have applied expectations to the relationships in your life. Will you do that?

1. Which relationship in your life is in the most

   turmoil?   (Marriage, children, sibling, co-

   worker etc.)

   _____

2. What do you expect from that relationship?

   _____

   _____

   _____

3. As you examine your relationship, are their

   expectations that are not being met?

   _____

4. Are those expectations of a selfish nature? In

   other words, would they make you feel better if

   they were fulfilled?

- *"Disappointment is a sort of bankruptcy - the bankruptcy of a soul that expends too much in hope and expectation."-*

-Eric Hoffer

Motivated by Expectations

The couple sat in my office. They were sitting on the same couch, but there was a pronounced space between them. She was upset. We will call her Mary. I had been meeting with this couple for weeks, trying to salvage their marriage. I had even shared with them the principle that I am sharing with you in this book. We had talked about expectations and how much they can ruin relationships. Mary had been giving it a try.

Now they were sitting in my office and Mary was angry. It seems that the earlier in the week, she and her husband had had a minor disagreement: the kind that resulted in him going to sleep in the car overnight! At some point in the night, Mary had felt guilty and realized how much she loved her husband, and so she set out to do something about it. She drove to a local all-night gas station and purchased her husband's favorite soda. She returned home, and softly opened the car door, without waking him up, and placed the soda where he would find it first thing in the morning.

So what was the problem? The next morning Mary's husband did find the soda, as she intended. If this were a movie, he would have drunk the soda, realized how much he loved her and how wrong he had been, and gone inside to apologize. But this is not a perfect story. In fact what happened was that Mary's husband found the soda, opened the car door and poured the soda out onto the ground! That was why they were sitting on my couch on this very day.

As I listened to Mary describe how upset she was by her husband's action I noticed something. Mary was telling me how what he had done made her feel, and how she couldn't believe he would do something like that, and on and on and on! Finally I interrupted and said the following:

"So," I began "if I am hearing you correctly, you are saying that you don't think your husband should have acted that way. Is that right?"

"Yes!" Mary replied firmly.

"Then I have only one question for you. WHAT DID YOU EXPECT HIM TO DO?"

When I asked her that question, she looked like I had punched her in the wind. There was that word! I went on to tell her that she had been describing an action on her part (buying him a soda) motivated by love for her husband. She had given it to him out of love, I suppose, but with a set of expectations for how he was supposed to respond to her gesture. When those expectations were not met, the relationship was in trouble again!

What Are You Motivated By?

The truth is that we are not so very different from Mary. We do things for people, supposedly out of a desire to love and to serve them. Yet in our minds we have attached a very definite set of expectations for them to live up to as a response to our service. Wives cook a great meal, expecting their husbands to be so grateful that they will offer to wash the dishes. Husbands go to work each day and expect their wives to gush with thankfulness for their sacrifice and hard work in providing for the family.

If you really want a good example of expectations, think about gift giving. How many times have you purchased the perfect gift for someone, and you knew they would be excited about it! Then came the day when they received the gift. You watched as they opened the gift. You could hardly stand the excitement. You hoped they would not be too excited over your gift, since you didn't want to make the others at the party feel bad. They opened the gift, looked at it, said "thank you", and went on to another present! There were no fireworks; no gushing words of appreciation. WAIT!!! You wanted to scream. You felt so let down! What happened? The problem was that you have built up a debt of expectation and there is no way the recipient of that gift could have paid that debt. You set yourself up for disappointment.

The problem with each of the previous examples is the problem of expectations. The husband who eats his wife's meal will probably not offer to wash the dishes. She will be disappointed. The husband who goes to work and works hard all day long will probably not be thanked for it at the end of the day. In fact, he may even get the cold shoulder for not offering to wash the dishes!

Whenever you and I do something for others, and establish expectations for their response, we are asking for trouble. They did not agree to those expectations. They did not say, "Here is what you can expect." You decided that. You expected them to give you what you wanted in response for your *act of service.* You were not really serving. You were making a loan!

We often fool ourselves into believing that we are serving others selflessly, when we are not. I had a church member tell me one day that she had left our church because no one appreciated the selfless sacrifices she had made for our church! If they were so selfless, why was she upset? She was upset because she had mispronounced a word. She had not been practicing *selfless* service. She had been practicing *selfish* service. She expected others to appreciate her in *her* way. She was motivated not by love and selflessness, but rather by pride and selfishness; the same way that most of you reading this book behave.

Love Does Not Mean Ownership

Love means service. Love does not mean ownership. Too many times when we perform acts of "love" toward others we expect them to be loyal to us forever because of what we have done for them. Every Pastor knows that that is not going to happen. Some of the people who have hurt me the most have been the recipients of my love and service. The sooner that you come to grips with the fact that loving someone doesn't mean you own them the happier you will be. When you serve out of love, you expect nothing in return. Love is a sacrifice. You don't get paid back for sacrifice. Are you really sure your service is motivated by love or an expectation of return?

I know that what I am saying goes against the grain. I have the same grain! When I do not receive the response I believe I deserve, I am tempted to get upset. Sometimes I do get upset. I stick out my lower lip and pout and say, "Nobody appreciates the things I do." Here is a question. Why did I do those things? Did I do them to earn appreciation? If so, I was not serving. I was *selfing*. Yes, I know that is not a word, but it is a problem! Listen to the words of the Apostle Paul:

2Corinthians 12:15 And I will very gladly spend and be spent for you; though the _more_ abundantly I love you, the _less_ I be loved. (Emphasis mine)

Did you see that! Read it again. That is so contrary to how we think it should work! Paul's love did not diminish; in fact it increased! Obviously it didn't matter how the other party responded. His love was not returned. He lost love! If Paul had expected people to love him as a condition of his love, he would have quit. Many people do just that. The Apostle Paul, while hurt at the lack of love returned, realized that loving and serving does not guarantee that love will be appreciated or returned. If you expect it, it will ruin the relationship.

Before moving on to the next chapters take a moment and answer the following questions. Again, be honest with yourself.

- Are you upset with someone because they did not respond the way you thought they should for something you did for them?
- What did you expect them to do?
- Why did you expect them to do it?
- If you had served them out of a heart of love and compassion, with no desire for a return, would you be upset now?

Chapter Three - Why Expectations Ruin Relationships

"I'm not in this world to live up to your expectations and you're not in this world to live up to mine."

-Bruce Lee

Life is not a Fairy Tale

Mary was a young lady who dreamed of getting married. She read all the books on how marriage should work. She prepared herself for the day when she would find her Prince Charming. She found him. Now, to be clear, *he* never claimed to be Prince Charming. He never rode in on a white horse. Still, Mary was smitten. You could have told her the reality and she wouldn't have heard you. Her marriage was going to be the best marriage in the world because she was marrying the most wonderful man in the entire world.

Without even telling you the rest of the story, I wonder how many readers will be able to figure out how this story ends. If you guessed that Mary was ultimately disappointed, you would be correct. I have often jokingly told my congregation that my wife didn't marry the Prince on a white horse, but she got close – she married the horse! The only fairy tale prince exists in fairy tales. Life is no fairy tale.

I don't want us to be too hard on Mary. I have seen, both in my own life and in the lives of those God allows me to serve, a tendency to place expectations upon relationships that ultimately lead to disappointment, disillusionment, and often the dissolving of that relationship. It doesn't have to be that way! You can have lasting meaningful relationships, but you will have to put away childish expectations!

I know that some may be offended at the notion that they have childish expectations. All I simply mean by childish is that we are not entering into relationships as mature Christians, but rather childish ones. The Apostle Paul noted the transition in his thinking when he wrote the following well-known passage:

1 Corinthians 13:11 When I was a child, I spake as a child, I understood as a child, I thought as a child: but when I became a man, <u>I put away childish things</u> (emphasis mine)

Children live in a world of make-believe. They mold everything around them into their imaginary world. I am not their Father. I am a giant living in a castle. Our family dog is transformed into a grizzly bear and hunted, with wooden guns, through the dense forest which used to be our living room!

We see little children at play and smile. We know their imagination is a wonderful thing. However, there comes a time when we know they must grow up and live in reality, not in their fairy tale imaginations. What does all this have to do with this book? Let me tell you.

In many ways our expectations are no different than the fairy tale world our children live in. They are unreal, made-up expectations. We are living in a world where everyone behaves as we think they should. That is a fairy tale. People don't behave the way we want them to. If I expect them to, I ruin the relationship.

Unrealistic Expectations

When it comes to the subject of relationship, expectations are one of the most damaging ingredients we can inject. We all have them. We all know we have been disappointed. Why are we so often disappointed in those with who we are in a relationship? The reason is because our expectations were unrealistic.

Joe and Sarah started attending our Church some time ago. They never actually became members, but were quite faithful to the Sunday morning service. Things went along quite well and I felt that our relationship was on good ground. Then one day a hardship entered into their lives. As a Pastor I reached out, and our Church also reached out. It seemed that we had done a good job of being there in their time of need. Then one day, the news came to my ears that they had decided to leave our Church! The reason? They felt that I as their Pastor had not done what a Pastor should do when someone faces a hardship.

Upon further investigation it was revealed that they had a set of expectations for how a Pastor should behave. I had not lived up to those expectations and therefore the relationship would be terminated – ruined. I did not know their expectations. They had never told them to me, yet they had held me to them. I went to the Scriptures and did not find those expectations there, yet they held me to them. Others in the Church felt they were wrong, yet they held me to them. It ruined our relationship and I didn't even know I had let them down until it was too late.

I could tell you many more stories just like this. You probably have some of your own. In fact, you may be reading this book, and identify with Joe and Sarah. Someone let you down. They didn't live up to your expectations and it ruined the relationship. That is what expectations do.

This book began as a series of sermons on relationships. I made the assertion to our Church that most people's expectations are dictated by their circumstances, environment and upbringing. Our expectations also are subject to change with our circumstances. For example, I have some Church members who do not expect me to make a weekly visit in their home. I have others who do. As a Pastor, it is impossible for me to live up to every member's expectations, because to do so for one, may cause me to disappoint another!

The fact of the matter is that when we come up with a list of expectations for an individual, and apply those expectations to them arbitrarily, those expectations are unrealistic!

God Himself cannot live up to everyone's expectations!

If you are like my Church, the above heading got your attention. *What? God cannot live up to everyone's expectations? He is God! He is perfect! He is all-powerful! He is all knowing!* He is all of those things, and yet I say again, that even God cannot live up to everyone's expectations.

How many times have you heard someone say they no longer believe in God because they lost their Mother to some disease and God did not do _____? (You fill in the blank) The world is full of people who are disillusioned with God. Why? He did not live up to their expectations. He let them down. They came to Him with a set of expectations that they arbitrarily applied and He did not measure up.

I say that those expectations were unrealistic. Why? - Simply because those expectations were not found in the Bible! We have no right to expect God to be anything other than what He claims to be in the Word of God. We have not right to expect God to do anything other than what He promises to do in the Bible. When you decide to expect from God something that is contrary to what His Word says, you are setting your relationship up for ruin.

Some people stop believing in God because He didn't stop their relatives from dying. Some get upset because they prayed to win the lottery and God didn't answer their prayer. Some people mess up and end up in jail, only to get upset because God doesn't bail them out. Now God may choose to do these things, but we have no right to expect it. We do have a right to expect God to never leave us nor forsake us because He has promised to do so.

I say to you again: Expectations ruin relationships. They ruin them because they are arbitrary and unrealistic. No person can live up to the all the expectations of everyone with whom they are in a relationship. The man whose boss expects him to work late once a week cannot do so without disappointing his wife: who expects him home at six o'clock sharp every night. Someone will be disappointed. Someone's expectations are unrealistic. Whichever choice the man makes, he knows he will have trouble in a relationship. Either his boss who pays the bills will be angry or his wife, who cooks his dinner, will give him a cold dinner and a cold shoulder to boot! Have you ever been caught between expectations? If so, you understand the impossible situation that conflicting expectations can produce.

I hope you are beginning to see the problem. Our expectations of others will ruin our relationships. You may be asking at this point, "Don't I have the right to expect things of others?" That is a good question. We will answer it in another chapter.

Before going on to the next chapter, ask yourself the following questions. Answer them honestly.

- Am I applying arbitrary, unrealistic expectations to those with who I am in a relationship?

- Do others know my expectations?

- Have I ever felt caught between the expectations of others?

- How did that make me feel?

Chapter Four - The Selfish-Hearted Relationship

- *"Selfishness is the greatest curse of the human race."*-

-William E Gladstone

Let me ask you a question. What do you expect to get out of your relationship? I am referring to the one that is in turmoil right now. Whenever I have two people who are struggling in their relationship, it is always because they are not getting out of that relationship what they expected. The problem is that most of those expectations are selfish hearted! That will be the purpose of this chapter. We are going to look at what it means to have a selfish hearted relationship.

Many relationships are doomed from the start because they are based on selfish hearted desires. We fool ourselves into thinking it is all about the other person, but soon we come face to face with an ugly reality. We are not getting our expectations met. Now we are unhappy. This is not what we expected.

Selfishness is simply the inordinate preoccupation with our "self". It is a desire for what *we* want, instead of what is best for others. As a Christian I realize that this is not the pattern we receive from the Lord Jesus. Consider this verse again:

Mark 10:45 For even the Son of man came not to be ministered unto, but to _minister_, and to give his life a ransom for many. (Emphasis mine)

Here is another question. What did Jesus expect to get out of man? The answer is nothing! He came to serve, not to be served! How many times did Jesus teach this lesson to his disciples, and yet they still argued about who would be the greatest. Today, His disciples still struggle with the desire to be the greatest, rather than the servant. However, Jesus gave just the opposite instructions!

Matthew 23:11 But he that is greatest among you shall be your _servant_. (Emphasis mine)

I can tell you that it is a rare thing to counsel people who understand that we are called to serve, and not to be served! Most of us believe that others exist to meet our needs. That is our expectation. That is what we believe we have a right to expect.

The husband who believes that his wife exists to serve him will be doomed to disappointment. The friend who feels that they are not being respected may feel that way because their expectations are not being met.

Let me go further and give you a warning. Often we fool ourselves into thinking we are serving when we are really acting out of a selfish heart. When you do what you do for others while attaching selfish expectations, you reveal your heart. This strikes at the very heart of our motives in everything we do for others.

In chapter two we talked about giving or making a loan. Do you understand the difference? Read the following verse carefully and consider it in the light of what we are discussing.

Luke 6:35 But love ye your enemies, and do good, and lend, hoping for nothing again; and your reward shall be great, and ye shall be the children of the Highest: for he is kind unto the unthankful and to the evil.

Did you see that? The Lord said that we should lend, hoping for nothing again! In the latter part of the verse he says that doing so is being like our Father, who is kind to the unthankful!

How do you feel when you do something for someone and they do not express gratitude? No doubt it hurts your feelings. Why did you perform that deed? Did you do it to receive thanks? Did you do it so that they would recognize your service? Did you do it so they would make you feel better? If so, your true motive was selfishness. The act of service with no expectation of return is true self-less service, and as such is a rare thing.

I can hear the objections now. *"Are you saying I should just do things without being thanked for them?" Am I supposed to let people walk all over me?" My husband doesn't appreciate it so why bother?"* These are all good questions. Let's talk about them.

Question 1: ***Should I really do things for unthankful people?***

The answer depends on your expectations. Do you expect people to be thankful? I didn't ask if you appreciate people being thankful. Do you *expect* it? If you do, you will be disappointed. Do you believe that you will one day be judged and rewarded by God for your actions? If so, your motives are important. I disagree completely with the idea that motives don't matter. MOTIVES DO MATTER!!!

Matthew 6:2-4 Therefore when thou doest thine alms, do not sound a trumpet before thee, as the hypocrites do in the synagogues and in the streets, that they may have glory of men. Verily I say unto you, They have their reward.
But when thou doest alms, let not thy left hand know what thy right hand doeth:
That thine alms may be in secret: and thy Father which seeth in secret himself shall reward thee openly.

Notice that the motivation of the hypocrite was to receive the glory of men, but why were they called hypocrites? The word hypocrite in the Bible is defined as "an actor under an assumed character". That means that they were pretending that they were doing good deeds out of love, when really they were doing them for the praise of men! God called them hypocrites.

There are a lot of hypocrites in relationships. There are probably some living in your home. There are, no doubt, some hypocrites reading this book! When you do good deeds for others out of love, then there is no need for public recognition. However, if you get bent out of shape because they do not respond as you thought they should or would, then you are exposing your real motives. You are a hypocrite. You're welcome!

I know this is difficult to swallow, but we have to face it if we are to fix the problem. The truly servant hearted relationship is one that doesn't ask, "What do I expect to get out of this relationship?" but rather "What do I expect to *give* to this relationship?" That is the difference, and that will change your relationships.

Question 2: *Am I supposed to let people walk all over me?*

That is an interesting question. Of course I am not suggesting that you give up all control over your life. I am suggesting that you on purpose decide to serve others. I suppose that may seem like being walked on. I don't think it is. I think it is serving. There may be times when you have to say no to someone's request for help. That doesn't mean you are not a servant. It simply means you are unable to help. Don't allow the fear of being walked on keep you from being a servant.

Question 3: *My spouse or friend doesn't even appreciate what I do for them so why bother?*

If that is your expectation, then don't bother at all. If, however, your desire is to be a servant, you won't mind not receiving recognition. Most servants only get recognized when they blow it! It goes back to motives. Why are you serving? Are you serving for recognition, or because it is the right thing to do, and God is pleased? By the way, God will recognize your service one day!

Hebrews 6:10 For God is not unrighteous to forget your work and labour of love, which ye have shewed toward his name, in that ye have ministered to the saints, and do minister.

Here is a task for you to complete before moving on to the next chapter.

- Confess to God the selfish hearted nature of your relationship. (Yes you)
- Ask the Lord to teach you to serve others as He did.
- Serve the person with whom you are having difficulty without any expectation of return. Let your motivation be love, and nothing more. This is harder than you might think at first. Pray and ask God to help you until you can accomplish this task.
- While doing these steps, meditate on the verses we read in this chapter.
  - **Mark 10:45 For even the Son of man came not to be ministered unto, but to _minister_, and to give his life a ransom for many.**
  - **Matthew 23:11 But he that is greatest among you shall be your _servant_.**
  - **Luke 6:35 But love ye your enemies, and do good, and lend, hoping for nothing again; and your reward shall be great, and ye shall be the children of the Highest: for he is kind unto the unthankful and to the evil.**
  - **Matthew 6:2-4 Therefore when thou doest thine alms, do not sound a trumpet**

before thee, as the hypocrites do in the synagogues and in the streets, that they may have glory of men. Verily I say unto you, They have their reward. But when thou doest alms, let not thy left hand know what thy right hand doeth:That thine alms may be in secret: and thy Father which seeth in secret himself shall reward thee openly.

- "The disciple is not above [his] master, nor the servant above his lord."-
-Matthew 10:24

The servant-hearted relationship may be the rarest thing on earth. In many homes and churches it is an endangered species. In some, it is non-existent. In the last chapter we took a good look at the selfish-hearted relationship. Now we will examine the servant-hearted relationship. I pray God that you will allow Him to speak to you in the next few pages.

The servant is a curious person. They are responsible for much of what is accomplished in the household, and yet they get almost no credit. In fact, they may only be recognized when they neglect their duties. The Bible again enforces this truth.

Luke 17:7 But which of you, having a servant plowing or feeding cattle, will say unto him by and by, when he is come from the field, Go and sit down to meat?
8 And will not rather say unto him, Make ready wherewith I may sup, and gird thyself, and serve me, till I have eaten and drunken; and afterward thou shalt eat and drink?
9 Doth he thank that servant because he did the things that were commanded him? I trow not.

Do not pass over these verses too quickly. Read

them again now. I want to point out a couple of things I often missed when reading these verses in the past.

- The servant in question had spent the entire day plowing and planting. This is no easy task, as anyone who has done so will attest!
- When the servant comes in from the field he is told to prepare dinner and set the table.
- He is not recognized and praised for doing this double duty, but rather is taken for granted, as that is what servants do.

Now, if I were that servant, or you, we might be guilty of at least a bad attitude, and at worst throwing a fit and walking out. But a servant can't do that. Please hear me out. In the day and time in which Christ was speaking of, these were not employees, but servants. A servant may have been indentured or purchased. Either way, they were not allowed simply to quit. They were servants. If they didn't like their task they could not change it. They were servants. Their life was serving, and that meant serving their masters faithfully, without expecting to be praised every time they did their duty.

Now with this backdrop in place, consider the following verses.

Galatians 5:13 ¶ For, brethren, ye have been called unto *liberty*; only [use] not liberty for an occasion to the flesh, but *by love serve* one another.

Mt 20:27 And whosoever will be chief among you, let him be your *servant*:

The verse in Galatians is a powerhouse! Did you read what I read? Paul is saying that in Christ we have been set free! "Now" he said, "you don't have to serve by law, you can serve by love!"

In the Old Testament economy, there was a law that said when a servant had been set free from his master, if he loved his master, he could voluntarily join himself to his master's house forever. It was just as binding, but it was a binding of <u>love</u> and not <u>law</u>. It was a voluntary binding and not one of necessity or compulsion.

I see far too many people enduring their relationships. They go through the motions expecting praise at every turn and performing their duties out of bondage and not out of love. These are the selfish-hearted relationships. The servant-hearted relationship is one where the individual voluntarily chooses to serve the other, out of love, and not duty; out of choice, not compulsion. No one wants to be in a relationship because they "have" to.

I do not know of a marriage where two people are married because they "have" to be. At least in America the old arranged marriages and shotgun marriages are a thing of the past. People today get married of their own free will? So why is the divorce rate so high? Simple: they enter into their marriages as selfish heart rather than a servant heart.

The same is true of friendships. No one is required to be friends. We choose our friends. If that is true, *then why are there friendships that are in such turmoil?* Why are you upset with that friend? Is it because they have let *you* down? How? They didn't live up to your expectations? They took advantage of you? They forgot some important date in your life? All of those things are about you!!! What about them? When is the last time you thought about being a good friend to them? I can hear it now. *"I have been a good friend! The problem is that they are not being a good friend to me!"* What difference does that make? I am serious! If you are miserable, then get out of the relationship. However, don't be fooled. You will have the same problem in the next friendship. You are the problem, or rather your expectations are the problem.

The problem is in how and why we choose relationships. We choose them out of a selfish heart. We subconsciously ask, "What is in this relationship for me?" rather than asking, "What can I bring to this relationship?" Do you see the difference? We ought to be looking for ways to serve, not ways to be served. That is the pattern Jesus left for us.

Understanding the difference between the selfish heart and the servant heart is vital to understanding the premise of this book. Why do you do the things that you do? When you do something for your wife, why do you do it? Do you do it to serve her because you love her? If so, her reaction will not matter. If her reaction matters, then you are doing it out of a selfish heart. Simple as that! A servant does not serve to produce a reaction. They serve because it is what they do. If they receive praise, then that is a bonus.

Again, remember the voluntary service out of love? No one made me marry my wife. I said I loved her and voluntarily committed the rest of my life to her.

So I serve her, with our without the praise. Why? It is what I committed to do!

I realize that this seems overly simplistic, but it is nothing of the kind. The lack of servant-hearted relationships and the prominence of selfish-hearted relationships is the reason for the divorce rate in America. We marry for what we can get, and when we are disappointed we leave. We expect the other person to live up to our demands, and if they don't, we are gone. *Expectations ruin relationships*! If we truly desired to love and serve someone, and recognized that we made a lifetime commitment to do so, marriages would last.

"But what if the person in my marriage changes?" Let me remind you that the servant in the Old Testament had no guarantee that their master was going to remain the same. Their only choice was whether to commit or not. Once the commitment was made, there was no going back. I wish relationships were this way today. Imagine the difference this would make in homes and churches if people were serving out of love and not expectations!

I will ask you one final time in this chapter. Are your relationships primarily selfish-hearted or servant-hearted? If you answer this question honestly, you will no doubt have some thinking to do.

Homework:

1. List the ways your friend our spouse has let you down._____

_____

_____

2. List the ways that you have let them
down._____

_____

_____

3. Have you been serving that person with no
expectation of a return? _____

4. Are you willing to ask God to change your heart?

_____

5. If you are willing to ask God to create in you a
servant's heart, you can begin by praying
something like this: *Dear Lord, I have been
selfish in my relationships. I have been living
with the expectation of being served. I confess my
selfishness to you and ask that you would create
in me a heart that desires to serve others, rather
than one that wants to be served. I want to be like
Jesus in my relationships. Thank you for helping
me. Amen.*

Chapter Six - We Need an Altitude Adjustment

-There are no easy answers, but there are simple answers. We must have the courage to do what we know is morally right.-

-Ronald Reagan

Read the title of this chapter again. Sometimes our mind sees what we want to see. The titles says we need and "altitude" adjustment, not an "attitude" adjustment. In this chapter I will explain the difference between the two, and encourage you to adjust your altitude. It won't be easy, but it will make all the difference in the world to your relationships!

I want you to picture and altimeter in your mind. Go ahead, right now. Close your eyes and picture it! Got it? Great, now let's get started. An altimeter is an instrument designed to show at what altitude a plane is currently flying. On our altimeter we have two words. At the higher levels we have the word **PRIDE** and at the lower levels we have the word **HUMILITY**. Most people, including the ones reading this book are flying their relationship planes up in the **PRIDE** altitudes. Great servant-hearted relationships fly in the **HUMILITY** levels.

Pride is a natural companion to selfishness. The reason we are selfish is because of pride. Selfish people want what is best for them, because pride causes them to believe they *deserve* the best. Selfish-hearted people expect others to do for them, because they believe they deserve it! It is their right! Pride tells them so.

The Servant-hearted individual flies their plane a little lower. They operate on a different plane (not airplane, but plane as in separate level: a lower one.) That is right, lower. Pride is up Humility is down. We naturally fly at the Pride levels. Humility takes work and an act of grace in our hearts.

You can try to temporarily adjust your attitude, but that does not solve the problem. You need to adjust your altitude. Consider the following verses about pride and humility:

Proverbs 18:12 ¶ Before destruction the heart of man is haughty, and before honour [is] humility.

Proverbs 13:10 ¶ Only by pride cometh contention: but with the well advised [is] wisdom.

Proverbs 16:18 ¶ Pride [goeth] before destruction, and an haughty spirit before a fall.

Philippians 2:3 [Let] nothing [be done] through strife or vainglory; but in lowliness of mind let each esteem other better than themselves.

Romans 12:10 Be kindly affectioned one to another with brotherly love; in honour preferring one another;

There are no two ways about it. Pride in a relationship will cause it to crash. Look at this one last verse:

Proverbs 29:23 ¶ A man's pride shall bring him low: but honour shall uphold the humble in spirit.

There it is again! If you fly up in the high pride altitudes, you will crash. If you stay down in the humility altitudes you will stay in flight. So how does this look in real life? Let me illustrate.

Tim is a hard working man. He could be any hard working man. There are many of them, all like Tim. Tim goes to work on time, works hard, and leaves work at the end of the day completely exhausted. On the outside Tim looks fine. However, you may not know that Tim is flying his relationship plane in the **PRIDE** altitude. Tim is proud of the fact that he works hard, and expects his wife and children to understand how tired he is. He works hard.

When Tim arrives home, he expects dinner to be on the table. He expects the house to be clean. He expects the children to sit quietly and not bother him, even though they have not seen him all day. Do you think Tim will get what he expects? Probably not! In reality, Tim will arrive home to a house where the dinner is not on the table. His wife will ask him to set the table for her, while she is cleaning up the chocolate milk spilled by their youngest child, only moments before Tim walked in the door. Grudgingly he sets the table all the while reminding himself that *he should not have to do this after working all day.*

After dinner, Tim tries to sit down and watch the news. He deserves the peace and quiet after all. His quiet is interrupted by his wife noisily cleaning the dishes in the kitchen, much to his frustration. He turns the volume up on the television. A few moments later, his son comes into the living room and walks right in front of the television to ask Tim for help on his homework. Tim replies angrily that he had better not be interrupted again while watching the news!

A few moments later, the chocolate milk bandit strikes again, by tugging on Tim's sleeve saying something like this. "Daddy, will you read me a book? Will ya Daddy? Daddy? Huh Daddy? Will ya read me a book Daddy?"

How much can a grown man take? Don't they realize that he wants some peace and quiet? Don't they realize that HE worked hard all day? Don't they realize that *HE* just wants to be left alone for a few minutes to himself? Don't they realize that ***HE....***

Don't you realize that all Tim is thinking about is himself? Before the night is over, Tim's wife is in tears, his son thinks Dad doesn't want to help him, and the little one receives a spanking for daring to disturb Daddy while watching the news. Sounds like harmony in the home to me!

I know; if you are like Tim you are already sticking up for him! I often feel the same way. That doesn't make it right. I can hear the objections now. "But doesn't Tim deserve a little peace and quiet? Doesn't Tim deserve to be able to watch the news once in a while? Doesn't Tim deserve...?" Maybe...maybe not. The Lord Jesus came not to be ministered unto, but to minister. He came not to be served, but to serve. He came not to get what *He* deserved, but to give us what we *didn't* deserve. He is our example.

Okay, here is another verse:

Philippians 2:6 Who, being in the form of God, thought it not robbery to be equal with God: 7 But made himself of no reputation, and took upon him the form of a servant, and was made in the likeness of men:

Jesus came in the form of a servant, not a ruler. Far too many people today enter into their relationships as a ruler, or at least royalty. They believe they are entitled to many things from the other person. Seldom do they stop to consider the needs of the other person, and that they may be in that relationship to serve!

What difference would it make if Tim would have flown his plane on the **HUMILITY** level? Here is how the evening might have gone:

Tim walks into the house and sees that dinner is still not on the table. His wife, who is cleaning up the chocolate milk, asks him to set the table. Without a word, Tim jumps in to help out. He sets the table and helps clean up the little rascal who spilled the chocolate milk. After dinner, seeing his wife is frazzled from a day with the children, Tim offers to do the dishes, and enlists his oldest son's help with clearing the table. His wife retreats to her bedroom for a little peace and quiet. After finishing the dishes, Tim sits down with his son and helps with the remaining few math problems on his homework. Finally, he grabs the milk chocolate bandit and sits down on the couch to read a couple of books. He helps the children get ready for bed, makes his wife a cup of hot chocolate, and takes it to the bedroom. After the house is settled in for the night, Tim falls asleep exhausted, but with a good feeling, knowing he has served his wife and been a good Father to his children.

I know…fairy tale right? It doesn't have to be! Let me ask you a question? Which ending would you prefer? In our relationships, the ending is often a matter of our own choosing. When we choose pride and selfishness, we ruin the ending. When we choose humility and service, our relationships are made stronger.

There is one last word of warning I need to give to Tim, or you, as the case may be. Be careful that you do not attach expectations to your acts of service. Remember, motives matter. If Tim had done all the things in the second example hoping for a pat on the back, he might have been disappointed. After all, his wife probably felt like she *deserved* a rest, so she is not likely to thank him! Tim's reward is in knowing that he has done what our Lord modeled for us. He has chosen to be servant-hearted instead of selfish-hearted. His relationships are stronger and he has grown spiritually as a result. You can do the same. The choice is yours.

Chapter Seven - Developing an Action Plan

-Any intelligent fool can make things bigger and more complex...it takes a touch of genious and a lot of courage to move in the opposite direction.-

-Albert Einstein

Okay, so you decided to give it a try. Judging by the fact that you are still reading, I am guessing that you really want to see some positive change in your relationship. Good for you! In this chapter I will be helping you to develop and action plan to implement this new altitude in your life. This action plan will consist of two things.

- A change in your thought process
- A change in your behavior in certain circumstances.

It will not be easy. Nothing worthwhile is ever easy. We are digging for gold. That takes hard work, but the rewards are worth millions! Are you ready to get started? Let's go!

A Change in Your Thought Process

This is the first step. Do not proceed to the next step until you have fully implemented this one. Recognizing that we are selfish by nature and that our relationships are selfish-hearted, we need to work to rewire our brains to think as a servant would. The following points are ones I want you to read, and then say out loud, then copy them down and carry them with you. Rehearse them any time you are about to have a relationship interaction. I know that sounds silly, but if you want to be successful, you will do it.

- The other person is not the problem.

- My purpose is to serve others.

- My relationships are not about getting my needs met.

- I have the ability to meet the needs of others.

- With the Lord's help I will seek to meet other's needs to day.

You might start your day off with this prayer:
   Dear Lord, I know that today I will be tempted to be selfish. I know that I have expectations that will not be met. Please help me to realize that I am called to be a servant, and to see the opportunities I have to serve, rather than the ways I want to be served. Help me to make other's lives easier today. Amen.

Part of successfully implementing this process is not allowing your thoughts to get the best of you. If you try to implement this process tonight, you will have opportunity to serve someone else, who may not be serving you. You will be taken advantage of. You will be taken for granted. You will serve without recognition. Isn't that great?! You will, however, have the confidence that your Heavenly Father is pleased with you, and the peace in relationships that comes when someone decides to serve the other.

Remember that it is a change in the thought process. Remember this verse:

Philippians 2:3 [Let] nothing [be done] through strife or vainglory; but in lowliness of mind let each esteem other better than themselves. (Emphasis mine)

That means to think about others as better than you. It means to prefer their needs above your own. It means to change your point of view from selfishness to that of a servant, looking for ways to serve; not out of duty, but out of love. Can you really see yourself as seeing your spouse as more deserving of being served? Hard isn't it? That is why it will change your life. You can't fake this stuff for long. It has to be a radical change in your thinking.

A Change in Your Behavior

Changing your mind is one thing. Changing your actions is another. However, let me encourage you. It can be done! You don't have to be selfish the rest of your life. You can have lasting relationships built on the model of servant-heartedness. The best part is that the other person doesn't even need to change! You hold the key.

Changing your behavior will be hard, but let me give you some examples of how you can put this into practice.

- Go home each day after work and look for the first thing can do to serve your spouse. Don't wait, do it right away.
  - o Do the dishes.
  - o Vacuum the carpet.
  - o Transfer the clothes from the washer to the dryer.
  - o Put the kids to bed.
  - o Make a cup of coffee or tea.
  - o Use your imagination…
- Study the other person in the relationship for ways you can make their day easier or better.
- Think about the areas where the most friction exists and ask yourself if there is a way that serving the other person could ease that friction.

It really is not hard. We all know many ways we could serve others. The hard part is doing it. Again, we are naturally selfish.

WARNING!!!!!

Don't expect everything to smooth out just because you do this for one night. If you have not been a servant in the past, your friend, child, or spouse may initially be suspicious of your behavior. Don't take it personally. You deserve it! Just be patient and it will pay off.

Don't expect them to praise you. They may not even acknowledge what you have done. That's okay! We are not doing it for praise; remember? Oh, those expectations keep creeping in don't they?

Do expect it to be one of the hardest changes you have ever made. It is tough. You are learning an entirely new behavior. Expect yourself to struggle, but do not accept defeat. Remember, if the Lord Jesus called us to be servants, He will enable us to be servants. Your biggest enemy is your selfish heart.

In Conclusion

Living a life of service rather than one of selfish expectations requires that you not give up expectations completely. In fact, you will need very stringent expectations. The difference is that you will be expecting things of yourself. Here is a list of things a servant should expect of themselves:

- *I expect myself to live for others.*
- *I expect myself to serve even when I don't feel like it.*
- *I expect myself to behave at all times in an appropriate manner.*
- *I expect myself to look first on the needs of others before my own needs.*

- *I expect myself to fight against the daily urge to be selfish, and seek to please my Lord, who was my example of a Servant.*

If you will read this list of expectations to yourself every day, until they become ingrained in your heart and mind, you will find it much easier to live the servant-hearted relationship.

-Courage means to keep working on a relationship, to continue seeking solutions to difficult problems, and to stay focused during stressful periods.-

-Denis Waitley

No one likes a hypocrite; especially when that hypocrite is themselves. I have heard numerous people say something like the following statement: "I don't want to go to church because I don't want to be a hypocrite." I can appreciate that attitude. However, it is the wrong attitude, and I believe the lazy attitude. If you know you should do something, and don't because something else in your life needs to change, you are lazy, or just don't care. Don't hide behind the smokescreen of "I don't want to be a hypocrite." It won't salvage your relationship.

Still, no one likes feeling like a fake, so how do we produce real change in our lives. That will be the topic of this final chapter. It is my desire to help you discover the secret to real change in this area of your life. It is possible. It is realistic. It will take hard work. It will be worth every minute!

I believe that no one on this earth is happy for long unless they are fulfilling their God-given purpose. Can you imagine a man gifted at playing the piano, wasting his life building houses? He would be miserable, even if he was doing something good. He would not be doing what he was gifted to do.

The same is true about those in selfish-hearted relationships. No one is truly happy being selfish. Why? God did not create us to be selfish. Our sin nature drives us to be selfish and sin never brings long-term happiness to anyone! If you are going to be truly happy in your relationships, you are going to have to learn to be truly servant-hearted in your everyday life. Are you ready to do this? Yes? Then let's get started.

First

Make it a matter of daily prayer. Ask God every day to change your heart to be what He wants it to be, and not what you naturally want it to be. Spend time praying for those with who you are in a relationship. Ask God to show you how to serve them today. Ask Him to make you aware when you are behaving selfishly.

Second

Meditate on Scripture references which have to do with serving others, and with the subject of humility. I will provide you with a list of references at the end of this chapter, but you should spend time searching for some yourself. Specifically look for ones that God uses to speak to you. Meditate on them in the morning and evening. Think about them as you go to sleep at night. It is amazing how when you go to bed thinking about something, you wake up thinking about it as well! What a great way to start and end the day!

Third

Make service a habit. Often our selfishness because a learned behavior. We may have a natural tendency in that direction, but when we reinforce that behavior we turn a tendency into a habit. For some people, selfishness is an automatic response. It has become a habit. The only way to break a habit is to replace it. You can make service a habit. Your old nature may have a tendency to selfishness, but your new nature desires service. Decide on some definite acts of service and do those every day until they become a habit. May I give you some suggestions?

- Wash the dishes for your spouse one day a week for three months. (husband or wife)
- Offer to fix dinner once a week for three months. (Husband or wife)
- Offer to vacuum or sweep the floors once a week for three months (this could be children, husbands, or wives.)
- Put the kids to bed one evening while allowing your spouse to go out with friends or just lock themselves in their room.
- Clear the table without being asked.
- Wash someone's car.
- Pay a bill for someone.
- Suggest eating out at the other person's favorite restaurant.
- The list is endless.

The point is not to make it obvious. Don't go home to your wife tonight and say, "I have decided to wash the dishes once a week for three months." She will probably wonder what you are up to. Instead, just go home one night and when dinner is over, offer to wash the dishes, or better yet, just start washing them. Don't say anything. If they ask, just smile and reply with, "I just want to help out." Or "I thought you would like a break." Maybe switch the day. The idea is to train yourself to be looking for ways to serve.

Now I can hear some objections. "Won't people take advantage of me? Won't they take me for granted? Are you saying I should let people walk all over me?" My response is this: "Don't you want to be a servant?" You have just described the life of a servant. You may get taken advantage of. You may be taken for granted. Someone may try to walk on you. So what!!! Our Heavenly Father will be pleased. I want you to think about the following verse in relation to these objections.

Proverbs 16:7 ¶ When a man's ways please the LORD, he maketh even his enemies to be at peace with him.

What could please the Lord any more than behaving as a servant? Our Lord was a servant. He called us to be servants. He was taken advantage of. He told us that the servant was not above his Lord, therefore we can expect no less. Notice that the verse says that when a man's ways please God, that man's physical relationships are affected. Specifically the ones that are in the most turmoil!

That is amazing to me! A man's relationship with his enemies may be improved by simply bringing his own behavior in line with that which pleases God!

So I beg you, do not throw away your relationships. Change your attitude. Become a servant. I believe that relationships can be salvaged if just one of the people in that relationship practices a servant's heart. Do not read this book thinking about how much your friend or spouse needs it. You need it! You have a chance to change your relationships. I believe there can be peace in your home. Do you believe that? Are you brave enough to give it a try? It won't be easy, but it will be revolutionary.

Do you want better and longer lasting relationships? Are you willing to do some radical rethinking and reprogramming in your life? Do you believe that God can change you? I promise that you will never regret putting the principles in this book into practice. As a very famous person once said, "I guarantee it!" Now go get em!

Verses on Service and Humility (KJV)

Philippians 2:3 [Let] nothing [be done] through strife or vainglory; but in lowliness of mind let each esteem other better than themselves.

Romans **12:10 Be kindly affectioned one to another with brotherly love; in honour preferring one another;**

Ephesians **5:21 ¶ Submitting yourselves one to another in the fear of God.**

James **3:14 But if ye have bitter envying and strife in your hearts, glory not, and lie not against the truth.**

Galatians **5:13 ¶ For, brethren, ye have been called unto liberty; only use not liberty for an occasion to the flesh, but by love serve one another.**

Galatians **6:2 Bear ye one another's burdens, and so fulfil the law of Christ.**

1Peter **2:16 As free, and not using your liberty for a cloke of maliciousness, but as the servants of God**

Proverbs **18:12 ¶ Before destruction the heart of man is haughty, and before honour is humility.**

Proverbs **13:10 ¶ Only by pride cometh contention: but with the well advised [is] wisdom.**

Made in the USA
Lexington, KY
01 August 2013